would   with   and

would   with   and

Cathy Eisenhower

ROOF BOOKS
NEW YORK

ISBN: 978-1-931824-34-7
Library of Congress Catalog Card Number: 2009935395

Cover photograph courtesy of Noelle Tan and Civilian Art Project.

Acknowledgements
Poems from this book have appeared in the following journals, books, etc.: *Abraham Lincoln*, *Dusie*, Phylum Press postcard series, Big Game Books Tinysides, *Ocho #23*, *clearing without reversal* (Edge 2008), and *Phoebe*. Many thanks to the editors of these publications and to the curators of reading series who invited me to perform this work.

to Ken

 This book was made possible, in part, with public funds from the New York
State Council on the Arts, a state agency.
NYSCA

Roof Books are distributed by
Small Press Distribution
1341 Seventh Street
Berkeley, CA. 94710-1403
Phone orders: 800-869-7553
www.spdbooks.org

Roof Books are published by
Segue Foundation
300 Bowery
New York, NY 10012
seguefoundation.com

Contents

My drug is myself.
—Henri Michaux

Premonition

this end like an ending quite unstopped
to leave the mantras room softly as a leaving
deserves that care, which I can't credit
to their selves recorded by a pen too fat
to make a very nice thing out of yours
or in English take the angles in which
our listing swims away from them, stop
the lists from such cadences

April in the Pink Sewer

Hello.

Where is my
mediocre
void

sting me to
drugstore
proportions?

I: a line.

Event: pulses along.

Rhythm: moderating fear.

I wrote
with a single stroke
in the margin
"Alwayswritelegibly."

Hello: where
do you go

Hello: let us go
to the danger

Hello: steel mill
rendered instant
in air

Hello: here comes
my void

flying from tree
to previous tree

Nohow.

my swarm-stung brother
ran right into
my brain at that time

first

       take your plastic
       machine gun

       break it playing
       at killing
       the neighborhood children

       stick it in the hole
       in the stone

the father with his
slow heartbeat
building scaffolds

house sold off
for debt

it was that lilac
time of year
when victims surface

Solid Figures Travel a Bee Line.

I thought (think)
I saw (see)
them killing
(that they are killing)
the man (many).

There is (not)
nothing to have (that)
but the ghost (chaos)
of branches
right through our livers (or)
(right through our endings)

The language (of bees)
is truly (begins with P)
the solving of (with)
the problem with (of)
the limits of
substitution

Forget (that) the m-u-r-d-e-r-s
or the being (too) close
to the sex of others
(that they are killing)
there is (only) one word
(that) you (in saying) say

Miniature.

I am prevented from
invading my

privacy, never
invited

to visit—maybe
it's the 20-

minute scripts & pitching
the jokes to who

the audience wants to feel
they seem—interruptions

that cause temporary
which is permanent

psychosis—& the fortune
to have my impulses, good

& evil, tempered
by laziness

and disenfranchisement.
I can never even find

the work of suffocation
among formats, growing

to know no language
save my own

Write-off.

these organizing
principles
hunger & money

push buttons to
& the project
manager moderates
my joy with
content with
this work in my ragged
patch
of vision

& so on & so
along sexless
parabolas

I donate my reason
to the beasts

in the books
around about me

let them wash
themselves
in the renderings
of themselves

Marble memo.

(I am not
committed enough
to watch a 3-
dimensional dance
of bees.)

how do you would
you break & how

a branch of

those branches passing through

the torso that belongs
that cancels out the dance

(In this case vision
is a tunnel
is a placemat
I put my eyes on it)

April Fools.

I knew me better
than you (do, or know me)
my warning turned

to a brain
&then said oh
&then took crumbling

pills (shut up.) into
my confidence
I always currently
cry when the world

opens (fuck.) the thinking
cannot find
my thinking belonging to (that's bullshit.)
who is this space

cannot touch the smallest
hole in the orbit
of exhalations
there is no above

there is no below
faces out to here
(yeah.) kaleidoscope
is home. I mean,
used to be.

La Marseillaise.

terrible terrible carrying

distance me vessel from the vessels

all I think about is
thinking about the idea
of how I can
get to be nothing

not a vessel
not hollow

like a kazoo

If I could step back.

if I could step back
emphasize my social position
with this eyeliner
communicate
what they tastes like
turn 38
you're a membrane
from death
seen selling meaning-
fulness at the lookout

if I could step back
look out
I've arrived at time
many travel to guess
at meaning
(I do)
destroying distance
with this eyeliner
sterile bunnies
found injected
with poems

I can agree as
a silence that possesses
neither corporations
nor god
look out
I am stepping back
the adverbs the
adverbs leave us
without quality

Say love & lie down.

To remain with the lion is dangerous
even a distant lion

can't
keep abstracting
lions, which is freedom received
virago & long beasts
happy to the letter

I do (see)
I should (recognize)
who dares (has courage)
per hour to say
to any me such
strong news

oh here is an apple
I found in
the lion's mouth

please ignore almost everything I said about
the little mythology that deepens the body
clayey as lamp agony burning of or with,
stock names for overlooking the floor of the cult
of the meal of the dead while growth into
on the town coins with iron, with quick
repression, with walls that serve as quarters,
tells a plateau to treble itself, make love
plural & bound by flaw—"that which will
have had spokes on fast fire" did not give as
blanket used to catch a falling object will

for you cannot know that except the stats
which the ramp made of brain brushes
which the gown made of men-brains they
grasp alarmingly for leaks
of the not saying it spinally out of sac
out of very nices and bilgewater pearls
as what act as high/low corks
thoroughly, vertebrally suspended mid-vessel
where their lies enforce precision of objects
relating to lack of objects (realm-specific this)
we were their "sorry to have burnt you down"
who to be seeming thinks it is good
to continue walking

nutritious the love toward registration whosoever's
midnight questions, like he's Balto-tropic
but madly this having to eat a meeting does wager
to mean what doing does to one through mouths as a group
or language/rails that terminate forward, they
who say would say "a kind of" future as in pend
as not in no arms to pen confessions of having
searched for seeing, the abilities suddenly forsaken
how can you keep your "lucky to have been the object
of screaming" away from refreshments which
when referred to hesitate in etcetera time, because
the infinite is a space too whether or not
you keep aware that way, as I do

how can angels have numbers in them
breaks toward edges naked amid juxtaposed
objects & abstractions that name you
as yourself, so why be described / accused
in the evening like that on the left where
it hearts yours through agreeable windows
proving that does loves her, for Free Will
is on deal with Yes, as in Did you
see (seem to kill) my house? as in
Should you not be (been to burn) without
a happiness? omitting the complement
is savory—its keeping of us in these
places occupied by "I shall not" &, vaguely,
"bought," a person can, which is, testify
via unknowing relatives

& make sure our existence still has roads in
other words, botch contempt as those such as we aged
in rotting barrels would when cornered by any
part of speech dangling through the grate like
that never sweetening *it* unless you play the
vietnam card habitually, an action marked
between how your face feels its suffix being
continued despite watching for durable outs—
a long shabby denotation, a singing astigmatic
difference, even a physical badness construe
us toward how to stop imagining which
being thought might please us

long live the momentary for there's
neither penetration nor a shot from a gun
to confuse the moral frequency with which
the eye factors passing facts to lesser organs
"I love you" is saying something more
to itself than termination of acidic tastes
incorrigible during the coming together
of matter never broken from the start, heel
of boot, cleft palate releasing sound into
the van as a tasty morsel. stop starting with
"this is universally noted," so's
the incomplete abandonment through which
we are traveled

I locked the wanting of the door as a soft
fish would in airing the room, found the feeling
of a landscape when persons not there re
arrange it with the goods allotted us
verbs turning to nouns out of habit forewarning
that which says as it absorbs watery filth
restrained by that it was a home for some
who look like ours but are not in thinking ours
nor could laughs mask revelations to the room
in mind refracting "tomorrow burned you
down for us" as though one
had stated its intention to return

of the eye also you receive receipts
a form soon being lifted in small amounts small-ly
repeated, as a day is, repeatedly lifted,
infirmity keeping the rooms huddled
but at large in the index to which purpose
the being at it serves (ever to option us)—
though thinking in the way turns grass
diacritical, something should would never say
"a refinement means a person who is licking
something said by should"
which we are all for when surprise at theirs
feeds ways to locate i.e. commit to
the us taken back to gone or fallen directly
that incision creeping open let them in

limitation as evidence of some light
that they await, when it is not there
in their known place though I'm not a girl
building model women reversed to want
the saying of them to happen soon,
her temporary parents sidling up to a box
of units, how many in a unit they may
be heard saying between breaths to discern
yours from the ones that were yours
it's not myself I invoke when I say that
to the drawer of forks, accepting tines as this room
full of removable faces

coup of the telltale toc not as in any
wire you travel painfully down, minding
our births dirty at vein level, so veins
that house the inability to help or go or
just eat a bag of its own food, which would
fuel the opposite of persons being governed by reading
romance into how the mouth forms you while
it sleeps, if does do sleep and mouth
what stands for creatures' flow
past objects eating the same that's eating
them, this is how breaks take you—
not cleverly, in the case of trained rats,
but uselessly, in the wakes of inflammation

about

he smoked himself across which shows him wary broken   und him
  [about is living alternate days of which there is no certain mention]
  decisions to avoid him in disgust with murderous plans that put the
  dedicated body into whose mouth is doing the killing of the mouth
  [about actually over the dead youth carefully studying subdivisions]
what a fantastic background to introduce why doubt is frequent source of
geography i.e. I cannot be complete about you   [how about survives its
  subject]   or little hims afloat in friendship words in place of feet
  those are not feet she was mating with   them mouthing scenic
language to your frag   [save one hate-poem for about to standardize
  approximate hate]   I war belonging to a thought and seeming to
  successive brains   [to stop about's rhythms and black foam]
all moveless queue   portrait of tracheas where lens touch skin   we
find work (equivocating) will do as jar us out of measures meant to bleach
        hands   faces
[about as indecipherable x-ray of a vegetable]   what do you use as air in
the two-inch field that is about the body   its place of origin conjectural

above

      ducking street birds as stuttered black-and-white   [contents of above
which feed on assembly]   born severally of cult and commerce   some
which disappeared backward—say I on the cry of the Whooper Swan who
attacked shadowy limbs within itself   [not cloud-high but close above in
range of touch]   no one died except the number 2   that sham beloved
    no fragments remain it being once or thrice for what you want as now
[above the years and murder lives a story that is killing nothing but above]
   as in beat your leather in the hot sun stopping to kill stragglers from the
truce   [how aboveness wages local victory]   the femurs buried in me
   move in scripted ways   carry various persons (or apes) and things
through non-dramatic blood   [above arms itself with hands for running]
floating heirlooms found in seas around my city   to correspond to more
than half of this   [there are stadiums in which to give above to many]
   who is the same person as the word for 'book' very rare and horizontal
others absorbed by birth float up as well   to leave a space for marks
suggesting 'love' on versos   [and that above produces very as a lostness]
   this in which conjectures settle found beside a boy flanked by wings
    things projected outward so flat they explain the eyes to specimens
[look up to feel above as it speaks itself in the crowd]   the oratory chains
    the markings to the sheep   whose touch derives regard

around

what wants you from me, that the wall is on   [occasioned as lapses of
  around, i.e. door]   —not startling switch but subtle mouth-cleaning
fumbles sound as escape from an ending projected   (that is projected
here)   on public skin   [around as that coming malarial day]   that
fountain there banished the town with a flock that bathed its victims in a
tube of light   [around viewless in the blood]   had been found by
  little love feeling to circumscribe the letter V and make plaintive the
  accountant of all this viewing   [the eyes of around age itself when
forced to view opulence]   V. who calls Professor of Love reaching for
                    burnt liver over the candle
[around against reminiscence had vacillating sons]   flickers over plush
       disgust found whole in every possible configuration

Things Made of Talk

&

Lay off the you
blasting furnace fur
nascent among tattooed double

helix for
the stinking stream of
them gone dry.

Father on the
mill Briar
Hill the knife so

blunt it could not
right the
severance.

sever queries from
the you drunk down
to level

men tattooed off
stinking blunts
drunk up

on the mill roof.
Fathers took their
scaffolds

gravel clicked toward
any you that
happens drunk &

doubled
over the briar.
You sever and

You blunt
the severing of
you caught

down the cold drawn no
money on
the roof or the his going off

to Arizona (and the)
fatherly with fur as you
tattooing mill

money the
gone stream gone.
Mahoning

River.
Sheet & Tube.
frost on the fog.

nightstick hand-
delivers joy
to the giver of

my dirty mouth of
that you picking
iron flakes from

every blunt
tooth thrown down
severed in the

frosty giver
econo-pathic *and*
will ever end

they say gook in the
turnstile of you
like money and

the and drive you drive
us mean deep
incision with

expensive blade soft
hand cut mean and
deep go father

briar ancillary to
Arizona drunk
severing fur

from tongue severing
and from greenback
drop yr change

down
the cold
river drawn under

Things Made of Talk

recreate pulling glass
            from proximate eyes

the mistake with
reference to the sun with

not the not seeing not
not the not thinking of the word no
not the not knowing of the word
                        how to stop

    the factory ghost talks calm & soft
                as we
                        collapse were buckling
                            under
                                home

    the tender
            awake

    the tender
                abandoned in the passage

        [now is not the time
            to feel]

descendant

abandoned in

juxtapositions,
                    (ear-to-eye eye-to-mouth)

adjustable crania punched out by
                    (many kisses stained blue)

abandon this sadness
                            (a while)
abandon my present lives
                            (secondly)

to hole up in the paint fact'ry
                            (she who will work will
                            give birth to
                            her own father
            (hand-to-mouth cheek-to-jowl)

she takes him by
                            (the eye)
            leads him down
                    furnace stairs
sneezing at
            the sun has had
            a name,   (force like any
                            talk is force) metallic

people
            people the
                    f-function of her (father)
                    his and is broken

early. no, earlier.

Elegy for Would

uncle elmer's empties back
of the barn blind & deaf

to lay me up in a hole
of talk to drown out
loneliness by a by-path

complications of synesthesia
drop you dead
or quoting sitcoms wholesale
in Esperanto (at this fusillade
of habitual actions)

put a prefix on it make it
mine over the knife
safely in my head
striking swarms
of the sugar-drunk

Elegy for With

turn your face
toward you died

on the way
from the government

there are usually
no characters

you just can't & the not
caring comes later

Softness of Persons Ahead

hallucinate faint
lull of the word
alequippa

holographic mouth with
fakes an ancient mouth that
hewn down to a sound for
where is the air, which was
around it, now

the micro-scopic void in my diphthong
that air was a father to me
that air was never in the picture
I tried stuffing it into my ethmoid
I hid the sharpness in my sphenoid
seeing is the last experience
our arms cut through
an absence of proof
all the reflex to
kill in my gorge

La blanche dame sans merci

practiced at head-
less travel low
society middle
fidelity who's
who of the re-
deployment
        line.

        (in the dirty hard chair.)
        (wavin' at the ladies.)

ass-ache of the pre-
pubescent money thought
us up & kept
its mind about us
oncet a week at
            least the hand-
made mannequins full
of the faithful let
me down into
thanklessness
(this is thanklessness.)

Photosynthetic

think he want to be
looked at
then seems to not

eyelash-to-rehash
how to render the seeing
right & make us

surface to endless
surface full of
tragic flaws the one

it takes plus fissures
inept at turning light
to food to botch that

resignation mouthing
fantastic appliances
attached to the mouth

out his stomach reclaimed
amnesiac devil's
strip who owns that

snatch of dirt oak
broke out of it
tornado death count

lower than he hoped
by several

Sinverguenza

not momentary
acts, habitual charming
with the lights-out voice
cause me to afternoon
squirm along the earth.
I did hate
them easy on
reflection times
we do learn slowly do
not learn away the men
driving men to their
going, the man you call
to wash himself in
the urge to cause
to come any
woman the
knife so
blunt & I wanted to
lock the door so many
other matters to
soften with myself

Sheet & tube

some wean some
water the river
dirty (me) to keep(ing)
that it was there
not in a good town

to fall upon with
stomach holes took
down from skidding cardiac
will it hurt yes a fucking lot
but till you die

—

is (get) bluish where
were ears with your
ears smothering thing
into which another
person poison bought

a little tube into which
one learns
to open enough eyes
say it does die
things to matter differently

—

useless necessity
marriage of various
vehicles—another person little
stick with which
I carry could

alleged candle under
candles soft of
use burning also flies
there's more than one
of the face beneath us

—

directly as a mirror
not accepting
all corners of
the room
shall soon return

rail without risk
it will may come
to us tomorrow with
when we receive it
yet begin to sing

—

concerning glass
with cannot go through
thinking was
spoiling history of itself
trapped on the other side

errors in transcription very
soft very narrow mouth with
(that once it was with)
out always without
ceremony

—

a swallow
swallows insects

but a leech
sucks blood

before

after awakened in the river as the feeling of bodied eyes   [before the
      physical's derangement]   afloat along a numbness called home
    [orations that caused us before they caused home]   which has entered
memory to collapse it into vast crumbs—this is how a fresh subject imposed
its systems   [talking of before to inhabit present action]   think (that) you
speak along the tongue telling nothing   [think before is that you speak of
your or other speaking]   these else to slip and spread in an altered syllable
    [can this be mimicked before you]   one falling alteration that swells to
occurrence as a presence pissing in the dressing room as well as not pissing or
    make a room a territory   [the seeing of it before it being owned   but
then before belonged to those who see now as well]   streams cutting it off
measure of awakeness—how rush thinking through to touch blurs that mouth
a broken   or saddle stages to the feel of that collapse   [never had such a
    knife as when I have before]   sum of fears   befores that come to wars
                    I cannot say flicker underwater
          water forced through organs does shed a mercenary light

by

      no such is thing to there touch   it of him (touch)   they of her (air)
    [then by door knocks some down to be witnessed]   eat houses all
    along themselves until the vein is titled dyed and very washed with
    hesitations kept as finger at a fragment's tip   this the vibrated life
    reaching bringing down to throat alone   [several soldiers touching
             each other warmed by by & imaginary fires]
that tells them liquid sinks beyond confession to neglect we target with
    fixed mouths & growing fixed beyond talk of some gesture flickered
    onto neuron walls   [then cause did legis bound by]   while with
    discrepant gait the boy strains for little throws of himself against
implosions invisible from the parking lot   [stick by excerpts' mind by
place by ruth nickling us down]   neighbors get involved with obvious
tattoos meant to approximate a poison year not yet on fire but as fluid
    doubling in the glass   [by sleepers they feign their location]   her
    flight a poison she prepared   there could be such a thought toward
             nearness though there is not

Premonition

do you feel with fragile, does fragile
overtake you (moving blood
as crux) when slow bleeds into
federal & people try to get you to
turn imagined suffering into twitches
"there's only one way to do this"
would prefer us but it doesn't
why does it fucking not
skin time when you can
as the little lung on my bird
quakes in attempt to use a word
possessed of so few letters
how to thing a thought so small
don't make you to breathe loyally
it touches for helping home not mean
you rake a vessel toward it

having injected topics where my cower
worked its papery dawn to pieces, though
this sounds foolish, pages caught
revenging roaring girls dressed to what
loafingly tackles the blurt of "theoretical"
twice-removed, almost by an already
dead his that was a cat who could
be called who, at they when difficulties
prosper like saying pieces into
the ownership's mouth, all what
makes the coming tears come and not
come, as the seeping grows vague
in its least brainward way

confronted in a surprising nemesis, enemy,
friend the all that you show goes away reading
itself among the plums yet to form over
headless offenders equipped with frailty leads
transparently theirs, though I am a scary
note tucked forward into the doings referred to
as yours, not filially drunk in the ways
of passivity differently keeping templates to
drink from

a piece of appreciated lining
turned outward was entered as
matter, linty long hair above as
well as sophomores ordering roast
horse's back pimpled by withs &
threats of satiation—a home
state to which return breaks
deletion into such sack that clicks
when it calls you (hello) from your setting
this from the collected stories
used by technology to impede, as receiver,
weakness (received), meaning nothing
much matters when rash
has you

when you're getting going one-on-one
with a bacterium that did in the wind
overpower the gone-home boat
still on the food in France, put, even,
subject to big occurrences of reigning
over uselessness, plan for tears to
shred you into blistery roots, use
a root as yourself, deny forms of
negative, privative, decapitation
viz. which of these at first wonder
does home in on its own hideous skin

to carry from the original place
generally restores violation's
stick to the not writing toward, sticking
to general, she more than girl than you typify
as a love list, as being useful in its
wig outfitted with happy eyes that show
the action has passed, retinally, remaindered
from a basin of dirty arm water
(not on the list of perfect
shouldness felled upon your length
which can be used, must be used)
having drunk the wire from your surface

unlike when you can instance saying
itself toward the very sort of thing protected
for use, remaining earthward, not showing
movement as toward does, or grind, here
it is confusion already running it in, which
bares the bringing of antipathy measured
in spoken names, hour that comes as you—
girl on a float, what would
creating confusion in our otherwise knife
with which path weighs each cost (is
so it is assurance that some not doing or
going might despise, imagine) cause, though
distinctions press little ideas into your beautifully
gouged palm lost like undoubtedly yours
and the asking of how many could
we not help not answering

instances of unwith did play us
two or three in budding towardness, what is
in the pointing of itself attached to that
Ohio that that man mildly stained, yes,
always it was two or only one when every
twitch born bland got softly fatal, eventually
observed from & of synapses such as
toward comes down to tell a thing
path does not exist, *path does not exist,*
though this event of measurement exists, soon
you will be upon observed receipts
as music's lost administrations

already beforehand returns turned into
having finished a strain toward "wish" or
"necessity," a list of what as soon as it
doesn't happen the apres-verbs are
teaching you—lifting weights, putting in
a waterfall, putting in a pond, putting in
a pool, putting in a driveway, feeding
the steel mill, dusting your going with
paths destroyed by the movement over
them with several eyes that learning
wonders over, as they had unexpected
telling to attach the should to the claim
made by the door locking love to gone

in solving for town the day'd edged onto
some self-referential congregation
symptomizing for long what the dog did do
to what the dog did think was the boy
until requiring specified units of time
to poke through specified skin as a mask
formed from below its own surface
don't disease the tell with won't or
categories that fit to won't
don't even adject cell to cell in that swollen
epidermal way you have about you

the circle does not touch (filling a dot to feel itself and) the triangle's sides
(another, hand-shaped geometry)   [telling it to stay like in stays or is
fondly put]   whereas here is hymn at the bottom of recall seeming's as
seem does sudden coming via wind and shaking his victims, trampling
every very flower without movement. movement from paranoia to the tem-
ple's gut   [in fears space while spanning significant weight being move-
less]   though private stopped existing. movement—as this is—leashed to
has to own. stasis at sea, at work, at least, at what harbors itself as home
displaced by killing fragments flashed by.   [broken that conventions of
the game adopt you   which inning claims]   what is the role to play, that
will play yours for the speaking of city, name, moral depravity expressing
how the tongue must be used for purposes that fear this stupid electric
flesh.   [imaginary skin and so imagined caesura shrinking to in what
holds a mirror to its back]   because instead of being composed for.
because with alarm for her own position. because drawn from many forms
of protest whose end projects pants-less taxpayers sniffing each other's gen-
itals on public lawns.   [framing being out of it with listeners could have
happened exactly away and going toward in]   as brief brides sail
toward magenta lips parsing a dead language   [turning to "vomit" via
expulsion from states of in]   the so-called intimacy of synthetics
eponymous chalkline this cannot go on. what is the theme of this, who are
the central figures, will it help to end the development of her story with
a series of bad puns on paradox?

& zones gone dead to force out the thought it was a man feigned dark
in the seer's brainpan, to was the thinking, event collapsed at disap-
pearance's edge even when built into human shape allowed toward to
deteriorate camp, breakwater, wall, encomia of bumblebees and salt.
[of as a child closed for any reason]   eye wheel half-understood to
replace the anus with serial refuges classed by sensation—correlate to
tongue, etc., fingerprint on the blood around his heart.   [what ofs are
spent upon, shot through with fucking]   that is how to think. that is
how to   to flee squeaking. not given the option that you may plant a
coin with a lung under the rare latter then wait for pleasure to roll the
garden into us.   [flinging themselves at the minute hand for of's
delinquency]   this line regards you as a separate genre, antidote to
stripping off the prisoner's clothes by feeding your regard, by
perceiving pain as ancient numbers meant for scrawling on a thigh, by
ligament all buried for drainage that keeps limbs free from recognition.
[egg-white savior of can carry across some rushing water]   does the
fromness that collects on you, spatula'd with hot wax over your pores?
do like perceive only like, strife passing in and love going out
via haphazard fenestrations?

A Mortal Handbook

mention not to
intend

mention it ran
away from me

(mention not to say that again, as well)

recount they did not live me There
There was nothing living to me

they happened to a Lot of Me

I can't say greatness in the case
of this family of speeches, not the fine
joke re: a portmanteau: you
when glad are understood
(like a ticket. like a ticket for a train.)

to start This idiomatically
when does starting travel This to the engine,
then look me pretty in the mirror

hold it
in place

to look at it,
your back to the engine,

or touch it repeatedly &
vary degrees of pressure,

does want tell them sufficiently well
what you want understood,

does it satisfy you so far from the station,
some length of time,

seven chances to get
less rich than ridiculous,

accept the room charged naturally
images into the tell,

with money
stuck to it,

photographs of me not wishing
to care perfectly, as the others do,

keeping talk vacant
on the off chance,

no, I do not like to travel
with one back to the engine

mention from me how preferring goes
his coining gun ideas survived by Theirs,
nothing but guns themselves
faces cut to ribbons, as is said
well I will take this Theirs from them
let us enter that
which registers kindness too late
to stay understood for long
no ribbons like that
satisfy Ours exactly

mention we have the right
reading any hour of day
accepting money in our rooms
beating down with weapons

this house does not belong
to Us, the people
in that house see Us in their books
which don't see back

mention we have no right to attend
as a mirror labors not to be it

mention to keep
out of red
paths to waking, love
to love disposably
mortals in the garden

mention a face has the red
path to human
given you weren't
looking are you
looking ever
as though I weren't
            a woman pasting
            joy into insti-
                        tutions

I said to make them
I had to say or they
would go unmade,
so keep out but
keep saying I
say to myself in times
generational

repeat this is a partial
house which path through
finds that it loses
capacity

tell the hand
        it's a book
wear helmets
        against metaphors

the question's ridiculous, "making plans"
he (thinks he) asks what explains him
that is not a moment, moving target, gun
        to talk me where
a line doesn't, cross me

mention not to attend
marvels prepared
to clear you, to sever I should
say, there I fear embarrassment
because I do not understand

to space things out
two lungs a brain
which nerves
cause telling

& what are they out of
their regular place, they are
exactly the weakest strong
of all, happened in attempt
to escape happening
a few feet away
the same remarks apply
to those over there

where we go was
driving over fire
as a quick
listen will tell, forced
toward the world I
cannot say was by me
as many things alter
the want to say the eye
has a sphincter, which
levels us

say soon afterward the subject of the verb
in which they both lived his,
to flower them while friends
saw it, I did see it, too, and thus
induced a gun to such an act
an insect of similar design belongs
here with a fine
antennae of sound
structure that buys
less than it weighs,
though little

say what should have made him
truth or told me to, ask him
(he's always telling me to),
where Going Away won't answer me because
were you to immediately when letting
answers want a place to go, pull out
a gun,
should not recognize
why simple trees
                    sold   Me
to other
less reasonable
objects

say to not say Or,
of all things
don't, it's just that

(empty
searchbox) nights
come too near
the throat this age

what wants wide
is etcetera narrow

invisible mirrors
suck Empress [dead ones]
out of live brains
Farewell, Empress

explain to the flinching face
      where it lives

e.g. "hey, you live under your own surface"

walking,

waking,

"Do you know what you're doing?"

"No. I know what you're *not* doing."

the only convincing thing left:
knees in the dirt

announce to
kneel as doomy
mood returns, never
leaves, came from
no resting place

dendrite
vs.
eating olives from a jar

this is where the end's
induced, great to be here, in your future,
thank you

(she felt
sustainable.
in the sunlight.

tell to make it good
for one thing

(found objects
in my sleeves

I could not
recognize

rigor
mortis

cells of
miniature
cities)

the money-box
is full

possessive
pronouns in this
mouth will
never leave

mention the greatness of use
don't mention

(& this a fear) I feel
too based in bosses
little stopping invoice
not fragment
not rudiment

so drag each
other down

say
strip down
to dead

make
honest
words of
women

[man, I love you but,
Fuck Off.]

suggest to
always take one
when it's offered

dissolve into
cobble, any
ground

that isn't death

find out how
to think it is

mention to not now recognize the act
speaking as a thing that dies, for it does

mean loving with their rooms in them
like yes replies meanly with should

without the seeing parts of garden brothers
walk to see well the walking questions, "big,"

look for Yours,
relate a story in reply
strong as a stick you would pay for

tell me away into some
other people who look
away from words. I would
learn that from them then,
perspective in a grammar
foreign to me,
even imaginary.

how it addicts
the world to us now
we have this
dress to cover ourselves from
their dogs at holiday,
nondescript as They
despite the angles.

Among *those* trees,
I am reading a book &
found an apple on the ground.
I see in a general sense
the objects, state that the sun
shines

Premonition

I go there, I am there, I talk home into coming
home takes me into account
as though saying "as though" thinks a thing
with no value, such as home
is it not normal to smoke a rainy road along
car windows while thinking pretends to replace you
with hate and owing hate go poultry-ward
without objectives that might could save
for later dismissal, pile of, the chicken softly
eaten in the way a door imports waves in
purposeful grasses—they in seeming channel
distance right to the retina, minding the tingle
that blankets hotly anonymous faces, when from
continued sucking all color reveals itself
facially, wet white opposite of cardiac

the and officiates, checks off behavior as its
enemy, inherited through loss of the right
paragraph, too much eye touching for anyone
to remark plainly upon without
the state of the stem, chew, a purposeful often
that hammers shape onto your little daughter,
which everyone has in the end, connecting
the tendency that has me in its stem, does
stem me into adding salt to something hunted
killed torn fried & bought & sold for objectives
not entirely applicable to most-often lists of mine

not the gone but the would go
downed me at the stranger brother
moving and aging in the received way
that tells you as it finishes, the having
told habit to measure truth again
tensing wire to not live compoundly,
among two threes and issuing steam
in which is does not find itself hidden
for theirs, constructed long out of differently
observed lengths washed of debts
in the coming snow sensing it will not know
to make water entirely bought for boiling about the doors
during reasonable love, willingly invited

as stronger brothers I would go to forsake
having gone, hidden measurements causing
debt to aged love's doors found unwilling
for old constructed reasons, not during
the boiling down of senses the steam
that observation houses differently in the soon
house about to be shelter, which mouths
how that particular bleeding makes us
the saying piece of "his will love my loving
of him," which can buy one anything

to-day in the evening the truth told her to me
as cutting what edges want into books
wrongs the fibrous purchase of how visible
offspring at a gallop can make themselves
certainly to eye them through hair-like
obstacles sleights ideas of courage, letters
long washed of sound unless, in carrying some
birds to the stove, our acquaintances accuse us
toward startles that act in our stead

it shall have come to me long to jam
long verbs beneath me, inertia near
the invitations piled like a series
of weaknesses undiscovered until
action is contemplated, I will go
away toward necessity, be used by dint
of homelessness that will have drawn
your truth toward anyone else's

the invited made-of-gold part of me will
always look to the yard that from then on
found somebody's heart beat two years
distant, this railway hidden in now's
countryside turned vertical, belonging
not to horizons upon the fireplace but to
being debt as a finding of itself blank &
shakey unlike a leaf for noxious bones—
now which wants to say me where my neck
expresses birds as they faint yet
quiver and devise instead of flying into

for whoever's cause (the nearer one, most
quantity of men of there, who from the said
words can still make other words never
heard to whom belonging goes), for whoever's
cause how I am obtained from the final
lack of throbbing, and wanting everyone
outside to continue, as your visitations
cease indefinitely of that place, of that time,
etcetera, and so on, for whatever cause
thought up to accommodate mystery
sometimes stopped by a heart esteeming
negative expressions, tying this not to that thing,
permanent to further off, for understanding
does not grow to seem washed or loved

for Mel Nichols

to carriers of gravity does matter be garden
whose invisible profusion rarely observed
could not kiss helping in exchange for
the canceling of color, anti-top to
anti-bottom, it is saying to everyone
nothing is dearer to nothing than
decay that produces very unheavy
light, not to plate experience in coins—
supplied by the negative lasts then firsts—
emitted as the constant being said as verb—
if should wishes us to like that alignment
then hollow hand with field, habit made hand

for Noelle Tan

a certain observation has made an observer
of some one thing that has had to have happened,
the watching of the falling put the body in that
stone collapsed to a single image, vectorless
I observe my closingness during many closings—
all with the least large tax on imaginary
values, as putting makes a chance boundary put to
the vanishing making about to be noun, verb, etc.
to which daily refers them, they with hard
wishes that occasionally manage to arrive
at three o'clock preceded by a state drawn
on the sense carefully, of their own ending

for Noelle Tan

where does itself find the door the yard
goes to fenced by an act as if tranquil had
constructed the window as well, clean
somewhere on its surface as attempts to
search unveil, which is itself and a finding
coat worn but not made by the known me
give us directions to accurate water accurately
so this project in some manner will seem
about to seem long looked for, not now so long
that you will have been washed of
accusations thoroughly built to pay me
leave, for some reason, exactly why
does not yet know me

something is the case, or
I see important you about things
of all the going back, of it all,
that what forgets me tells
hard approaches to approach your things
that lie about me until which time
they keep my feet from touching
land, there is no such voice
underfoot—I want to say only but
rather say I want to say it

thread is plucked many days for us
you have plucked it
magnetic clouds they are real
clouds of objects throated oval box
it isn't that the talking coming makes
a camera of her wife
though to repeat those silences
she saw the field of rooms remain
about her torso

the splinter is one
in a sense, I say something
is the case, you say
something is the case
I try to think to speak
so call the Future Poets of America
who kill bronchial moments by
burning candles on a face
better to wash than melt a town
we feel mostly with our feet
perception given way to blinds
then a list of other words
believed to soon be coming

on

to find where I treat you as having extension that touches this   soon rebuilt
me   not nothing an excavation that turns the surface under until a buried
wire causes us to flinch and weave away toward the other burnings.
[bringing on to facial levels down]   the house was artificial evidenced by
blood the light is driving through to project a peninsula overhead.
[possess a surface to feel this on]   which organ of your body grinds
against the ground as though compressing a tangle into an instance,
how will machine sub us out—the brain enclosed, itself cared for based on
someone else's silence, someone else's dirty boat between the crop marks.
[so cannot look at soon as on's reveal]   as the friend in need a policy puts
us in our places characterized by blue-sky greetings and seldom sensations
intensified to the purely alleged. why does the coursing seem external to
xanthan gum out of proportion to what the end of loveliness requires—
cruelty points to empty because it does turn into namesake tree where to
bury the unburned as the very shiverers under our own shorn hair.
[there's a moving of on toward metaphorical foreheads]   hence gets to be
said don't give us a choice between this or this becoming an
artificial cave made of mourners' heads.   [on holy not to touch the]
little framed weeping. lie on this couch. that is a day you are staining
to describe you.

out

keep it, just keep it there, symbol couched as mistaken for prose.   [out the
   safer keeping place that comes to time us]   the running left its water
without from the back and forth across domestic surface.   [water unable
to claim escape from vacuoles]   particular stones here are for in wet
pockets newly made of flesh—when the veins these five days and the liquid
      part absorb from foreseeing liquid cultures exhausted but friendly.
      [in refusing out I strand proof amid brochures of human capacity]
   the purple day with anus stormed the city or sat upon it, left a purple
border to be opened as soon as it dried.   a very dark while in the field.
[out holds me frantic away from that image of my image in the field—there
was image in the field]   the bus times propose rituals to where the retina
denies itself, evacuates itself with no thought of such factors as evidence or
motive.   [out grows hungry with the work of tautology]   there mind is a
not there wall degenerates into garment for the spleen the moment it refutes
   its hostage fact, maybe it always will.   [out it again which piece still
reflects its time in]   by her by means of a fiction, an armored war-dance
performed with eyes and mouths and clasping hands over snakes drawn
over a flame.   [enter trance to say trance the location of which arose from
the prison wall]   I am usual in winter taking the places of earlier forms of
   promise and therefore the sentiment ends with snow landing on a dried
      organ now suitable for kicking. don't let it move toward me. please.

the point oft touch goes invisible when door will not provide itself to such flames, as
dimensions limit geometry to a small quality tinged with collapse into cardiac.
[at disguises lapse as equilibrium—no relation quells the building of mouth, the
watching of the building of mouth via murmured projections]   I find approach
settling into a hand partially mythical, bitter over lost exhaustion when that is a dearth
of cellular gravity needing vast motions beneath it by having them ad finitum.
[your will will meet at as candidate for extraneous organs]   to want to cause need
out of their own bodies,   [there is relation basing at on fertile nubs that double as
turns of mind a lurch toward stimulation]   in binding 'love' to sodium benzoate, in
stinging with your tongue a scorpion through its carapace, in contagious spirits living
under the nail enough to turn flesh into war shown for the raw toward of exaggerated
oracles.   [we are at fault more than at destruction by the it being only natural, time
found to take us to the rain which for once relieves]   counting the stakes and the
phallus's charms do grant fire the capacity to measure possible distances. and in a
private curse of during or after it inches into the company, more reason to kill it then
invent it by describing gruesomely it—you make an image of a person whose love you
desire or whose death you wish, you melt it with a fire, you pierce it with nails, etc.,
mostly it speaking you away from what was called 'earlier' in the solving of
description. the door bursts a wind open as can force the lung originates, science of
lies, there is no proximity more terrible than the silted up window overlooking itself.

Ass

Film

[This films "I can say that," "I can suggest it," "I can say that." Will it—pass on a splotch—color the duct of between with space and god with impure deadly blue physically stained into glass. Nothing is really a question (recorded love on phone I do not love says nothing's invisibly wrong— response to myth that body exists), is it? Sample this natalician camera replacing light with my mouth, no authority or meaning, and nothing new when worded in sober order. "Head" becomes "Belief." Red stain comes into focus. (Oh it's a human organ.) Obsolete sex as the price of numbers causes what we say to happen—flicker—flat—imitation—cunt pried open. I can be funny, too, like a member of death renderings privately screened. Fuck you I am funny. The humor is hilarious in its absence. Dogs, horses, nets, and traps, the poem breaks off on the verge of the chase. Don't be stupid [hit head], this is not a film. This is nothing. Feel too seriously and too serious. The bathroom recolonized with yellow lotions—surround sound growing a monstrous body whose diction extends to your crotch and takes up entire screens. People with words and mostly faces mouth "I know what that means." Software. Real air. Other unoriginal voyages. I came here to party or got here thinking how small knowledge is so let's beat him up with this saucepan then pour sauce over his genitals. Judy did that in Oz and they cut the scene.]

[Needle approaches neck. [Turn away if you can—it's a neck unless we abandoned dimension in time, or were abandoned by it, or abandoned ourselves. File for a patent on this particular sourceless extended psychic pain that causes twitches and other deliria, punctuation on a gland that appears as a full stop on film. Virgil abandoned us with our children now no more stories to make the torture coherent. Things to do: eat a timorous state, spit out the sinews, flee to the small, dark, uncomfortable place of our descendants. The mercy-tempered metal buried in your head.]]

for April Caskie

Ass

fine thought illumines ass [& asses].

sniffing trust freshly helmed, escaping wrought as ear where mouth should have sung [sang into].

the part about particulars made us lock our eyes in the safe [for far-spoken young (at 2:34 pm) animals].

between keystrokes touch desert ointments—that tame causes—that frail repeat—that fail to enter what stands for these [of which I am part].

o

tiny iridiscent noise wreaked the face deaf.

white as dots micro contact at hints of large sex havings.

lemon on one once rolled hole-ward.

at the untelling at the hole—content.

at 1:47 pm, at those saying in them to chew harder on the hair.

o

am is constructed of mags when wanting to be.

ass not funny on approach.
app as roach, menny legged.

assy barrage.

tiny assy map-on is ass that touch mythy corneal feelers while whitenessing.

eery descent to table, music, 2:26 pm, funicular lament that teaches stop.

pluck.

system center. & speed. & should from not. & feeble gait to after.

o

somewhere there's music killing ass feelings.

6:42 pm.

to kiss to lick to sense to hurry to receive the quiet splice at once.

[I changed kiss to kick and lick to kick and sense to kick and hurry to kick
and receive to kick the quiet splice (changed to kick) at once.]

with several yous at proper angles, their ass nebula kicking those ears sewn
shut.

o

& shut my doe-eyed ass precisely.

lobsterfuge, dumpsterfuge.

frugal falling of black hair shafts into the pool around the wick. (this sounds like something being said.)

saved by me, 6:36 pm, as clump the demo into gagging toward voiding organs meant to void, awash.

work, fledgling, foundling, crevasse, sentimental lushness, green prick is choose distinctly shadowy spaces.

o

into burden whence language, ass né Ibid. a-pon loud shalls must clear.

that wants to say that & be placed there, feel the placement of me there, the placing act.

wheel water drains from a bray
when pure light finger far from brays
whose hairs on fire quote starres rightly & enter it
which bridges back us to empty lions
wedding luxury to the bearing of frantic whore
ass, mine.

6:03 pm

o

one night acts as a government wants me to act, like an 8:03 am, fish fights in the second throat instead of smoking dares for mine.

what this vocab produces grafts the purest milky long ago.

flashing ethnologists lation, very stately *groserias* felt by they would asking say to refuse to tell what states came out onto the flatbed, bloody denim, ass-based correlations.

the universe ordered me to say *dick, tits and ass,* and, finally, *wet vagina of solidarity.*

gringa whore is said to prod the chief hello, they wanted to know how holding anecdotal cunts in high esteem trails them from her doorstep to the next house & the next house & then also the next.

my ass is a product of the crowd you fell in with.

please indicate you understand the words that go with this.

and give me your sister. good morning.

o

turn to face the viewer.

tweak the other's nipple.

rape as a gift painted into the postures.

rape as a *gift* painted *into* the *postures*.

notorious tub of young friends there to keep from stating—say hell to them.

we feel so full of mostly unusable luck at 5:46 pm.

cite just three examples of anything known as snuffbox.

crammed with hair, tiny, abated mirror that is very touching this early.

mouth to labyrinth, the letter's croak a rake scraped over the organ.

o

recast ass broader and deeper.

define mobile ass geography, minute lapse between them, caking.

your ass edges toward five feet from other asses at 6:02 pm.

parts of them touch fabric, break fabric, erupt onto fabric, shift fabric.

there the notable eyelid turns to scissors for social firsts.

you think of ass as funny.

it is in words, untender distance, are always, are having caught up, are always faces undergoing faces.

o

we rapes stick together via literal genital contact.

you let the least of your body touching the floor found a field, race to little states that enter such regard as this.

grid, grit, grin, grill [but here eye level kills them with familiar, mustn't tighten toward brain in the vessel, precisely].

I want to begin to be regarded as war.

as 3:22 p.m.

my very is general, facial technologies, they do so for force forces them to.

the movie at multiple durations to move along a line, along a line, along a line.

o

stress the array—the system of the porosity of of.

ass tax was no longer to be overwhelming murderous harmonies, as felt becomes factory, producing waves, vessels, handles, simple commands, tinges on the nonce edge.

I sued to think of visiting with the need to get beyond this day, visiting a person to say a person seems plausible, need for particular touching, touch me "she" say, "she" say "she" call him up, "she" say "he" two blocks away, "she" put herself into play must put different parts of herself into play toward a blank situation.

as felt relies very well on data, so beds were made to be described as furniture, lumpen as we work to get more dresses.

an order in the pointy organ, inward, flow-ers disguised as hairs glued to the slide.

what time is it.

it's 1:28.

ROOF BOOKS

the best in language since 1976

- Arakawa, Gins, Madeline. **Making Dying Illegal**. 224p. $22.95.
- Dworkin, Craig, editor. **The Consequence of Innovation: 21st Century Poetics**. 304p. $29.95.
- Gordon, Nada. **Folly**. 128p. $13.95
- Guest, Barbara. **Dürer in the Window, Reflexions on Art**. Book design by Richard Tuttle. Four color throughout. 80p. $24.95.
- Fitterman, Rob. **Rob the Plagiarist**. 112p. $13.95
- Nasdor, Marc. **Sonnetailia**. 80p. $12.95
- Perelman, Bob. **Iflife**. 140p. $13.95.
- Price, Larry. **The Quadragene**. 72p. $12.95.
- Reilly, Evelyn. **Styrofoam**. 72p. $12.95.
- Shaw, Lytle, editor. **Nineteen Lines: A Drawing Center Writing Anthology**. 336p. $24.95
- Sullivan, Gary. **PPL in a Depot**. 104p. $13.95
- Torre, Mónica de la. **Public Domain** 104 p. $13.95.

ROOF BOOKS are published by
Segue Foundation
300 Bowery • New York, NY 10012
For a complete list of titles visit our website at **seguefoundation.com**

ROOF BOOKS are distributed by
SMALL PRESS DISTRIBUTION
1341 Seventh Street • Berkeley, CA. 94710-1403.
Phone orders: 800-869-7553

spdbooks.org